AF679527

The 15 Rules of Money

Jackson Cooper

Copyright Page

Copyright Holder: © Jackson Cooper
Author: © Jackson Cooper 2025
Publisher: Dakini

Index

Money is not spent, it is multiplied

From a young age, we were taught that money is meant to be spent. That you work, you get paid, and then you spend it on whatever you need. And if there's anything left over, well, great, you save it. But no one told us that money can also multiply. That it's not just used to pay bills, but can reproduce itself. And not with magic, but with smart decisions. The most common mistake people make is to view money as a finite resource: you have it, you use it, and it's gone. But those who truly understand how the money game works see it as a seed. Not as something to be consumed, but as something to be planted.

Spending money is easy. You buy a new cell phone, pay for dinner, treat yourself. And yes, it's okay to enjoy yourself, but if every dollar that passes through your hands goes toward things that leave you nothing in return, then you'll never have financial stability. Because what matters isn't how much you earn, but how much of that money stays working for you. Imagine if every dollar you earn could become a little worker. If you spend it, that worker disappears. But if you invest it, it starts producing for you. And over time, it brings you more money than you initially invested.

Multiplying your money doesn't mean becoming a millionaire overnight or taking crazy risks. It means having the right mindset. If you get an income, before thinking about what you're going to spend it on, ask yourself: How can I use this money to earn more? Sometimes the answer lies in putting it into a simple investment. Other times, it lies in acquiring a new skill. Sometimes the best investment is a course, a book, or a tool that makes you more productive. The important thing is that this money doesn't die as soon as you touch it. That it has a second life, a use beyond consumption.

The problem with seeing money only as something to be spent is that you fall into an endless race. You work to earn, then spend to live. And so on, month after month, year after year. There's no real progress. You're just running on a wheel that never stops. But when you start using money to multiply, something changes. You start buying assets instead of liabilities. You start building, not just consuming. And, over time, there comes a point where your investments generate income without you having to work as hard. That's the real goal.

Most people aren't poor because of what they earn, but because of what they do with it. You can have a good salary and still live on the edge because everything that comes in goes out. Meanwhile, someone with a modest income but a multiplying mindset can gradually build a much more solid future. The key is how you think. If your mind is trained to spend, you will spend. If your mind is trained to multiply, you will become more skillful, smarter, and freer over time.

It's important to understand that multiplying isn't always immediate. It's not about getting rich in a month. Sometimes the best financial decisions take time to bear fruit. But that doesn't mean they aren't working. A tree takes time to grow, but when it does, it provides shade for many years. That's also the case with well-planted money. Maybe you make a small investment today, but in a few years, that decision can give you life-changing income.

Even the little things count. If instead of spending ten dollars on something unnecessary every week, you decide to put it into an investment, into savings that actually gives you something, you're practicing this rule. You don't need thousands to get started. You need awareness. Every spending decision is an opportunity to multiply or to lose. Every time you choose to spend on something that doesn't give you anything in return, you're giving up that possibility of growth. And if you repeat that every day, you end up trapped in a life where money always slips away.

Multiplying your money also forces you to think differently. Instead of seeking immediate pleasure, you begin to value the future. You learn patience. You learn to see money as a tool for freedom, not just a means to buy things. That mindset changes everything. It's not about being stingy, it's about being strategic. Spending less isn't living less; it's living with purpose. And when you see the results of your smart decisions, you begin to enjoy a peace of mind that compulsive spending will never give you.

So the next time you have money in your hand, don't think about spending it. Think about how to make it come back to you. Ask yourself if you can turn it into an asset, an investment, an improvement. If you can do that, even with a little, you've mastered one of the most powerful rules of money. Because money isn't meant to disappear, it's meant to grow. It just needs you to understand it that way.

Spend Less Than You Earn (Always)

One of the oldest rules of money is also one of the most ignored: spend less than you earn. It sounds simple, even obvious. But if it were, most people wouldn't be in debt, stressed, or living on the edge of their income. It's so basic that it's underestimated. But this rule, properly applied, is one of the most powerful there is. Because those who spend less than they earn always have control. They have leeway. They have room to breathe, to decide, to avoid falling into despair when things go wrong.

The catch is that, as incomes rise, many people also upgrade their lifestyles. If they earn more, they spend more. They upgrade their cell phone, their clothes, their car, they eat out more often, they indulge more. And over time, even though they earn more, they're still where they started. There are no savings, no investments, no cushion. Just a higher income and equally high spending. It's like filling a bucket with a hole in the bottom: no matter how much water you put in, it always leaks out.

Living below your means isn't synonymous with poverty. It's synonymous with intelligence. It's understanding that the money you don't spend is money that can give you peace of mind, freedom, and opportunities. Those who live right on the edge of their income are on a tightrope. One layoff, one illness, one emergency, and everything collapses. There's nothing to hold them up. On the other hand, those who spend less than they earn have a cushion, a shield, a protective barrier. They're prepared for the unexpected.

Now, it's not about living like a monk or giving up everything you love. It's about having priorities. Learning to differentiate between what you want and what you need. Not letting impulse decide for you. Because if every time you have money you let yourself be driven by whim, desire, or social pressure, you'll fall into the same old pattern: work, get paid, spend, repeat. And that gets you nowhere.

When you learn to spend less, you realize that many of the things you used to buy weren't so necessary. You realize that you can live well with less. You often bought things out of anxiety, boredom, or just wanting to fit in. Conscious spending changes your relationship with money. It makes you stronger, more confident. Because you know you're in control of your finances, not them in control of you. And over time, that habit becomes a tool of power.

A useful trick is to set a fixed percentage for spending and another for saving. For example, you decide you're only going to spend 70% of what you earn, and you'll use the rest to save or invest. At first, it may seem difficult, especially if you're just spending it all. But with small adjustments, you can achieve it. Maybe you stop ordering takeout so often. Maybe you postpone an unnecessary purchase. Or you cancel a subscription you don't even use. Little by little, your spending will adjust. And at the end of the month, seeing that you have something left over becomes a huge satisfaction.

It's also important to keep track. If you don't know where your money is going, you won't be able to correct anything. Recording your expenses, even in a notebook or using an app, opens your eyes. You discover that you spend more than you thought on certain things. That there are leaks. And when you see them, you can close them. No one gets rich without knowing how they spend. People who control their money do so because they have the habit of scrutinizing every penny that comes in and goes out. It's not an obsession, it's responsibility.

When you spend less than you earn, you give yourself permission to dream. Because now you have the resources to build something. You can save to travel, study, start a business, or simply live more calmly. Financial anxiety disappears when you have a margin. And you don't have to earn a fortune to achieve it. What you need is discipline, clarity, and consistency. Those three things are worth more than any pay raise.

Financial freedom doesn't start with earning more. It starts with spending less. Because if you don't know how to manage a hundred, you won't know how to manage a thousand either. The problem isn't the amount, it's the habit. And this habit can be trained. It starts with small decisions. One day you decide not to buy something you don't need. Another day you cook at home instead of going out. Yet another, you choose to wait before making an impulse purchase. In this way, day after day, you build a new way of relating to money.

This principle is so powerful because it can be applied at any time. You don't need to have much to start. You just need to decide that you're going to live on less than you have. And when you do, everything changes. You stop being a slave to the next paycheck. You stop running after money. You start making decisions from a place of calm, not from need. And that, in the end, is what makes the difference between a life of debt and a life of freedom.

Save as if you Were Going to be Left with Nothing

Saving isn't boring. Nor is it something you do only when you have extra money. Saving is an act of intelligence, of anticipation, of self-love. It's like packing a backpack with water before crossing the desert. You don't know how far you'll walk, or what will happen, but you carry water because you know you'll need it. That's how saving works. It's that silent backup that goes unnoticed when everything is going well, but turns to gold when things get tough. And that's why you have to save as if one day you'll be left with nothing. Because at some point, perhaps not so far in the future, that may happen.

No one is immune to emergencies. You could get fired, there could be a crisis, an unexpected medical expense, an opportunity that requires immediate cash. And if you don't have savings, you're trapped. Dependent. With no room to maneuver. So the first thing you do is borrow, use your credit card, go into debt. And so begins the cycle that's so hard to break. Those who save, on the other hand, protect themselves. They have options. They have power. Because saved money isn't just money; it's time, peace of mind, freedom.

Saving as if you were going to end up with nothing means having a preventive mindset. Don't wait for trouble to arrive to start taking care of your finances. It means saving even if you earn little, even if you feel like it doesn't make a difference. Because it does. Every penny you don't spend and that you save intentionally builds an invisible wall that defends you from chaos. And if you do it consistently, that wall becomes strong. Strong enough so that if one day everything goes dark, you'll still have light.

Many people say they can't save because they don't have enough. But often it's not a question of income, but of habits. The problem isn't how much you earn, but how you distribute what you earn. If every time you get paid, you already have in mind what you're going to buy, where you're going to go out, or what you're going to renew, then you're not prioritizing the future. You're letting the present consume everything. And if the present consumes everything, the future will always be uncertain, weak, and full of fear.

Saving doesn't have to be large to be useful. Sometimes saving is simply not spending. Choosing what's necessary. Letting go of something today to have something better tomorrow. You can start with the bare minimum: 5 percent of your income. Then 10 percent. The important thing is consistency. Every month, without fail, leave a portion of what you earn untouched. Store it as if it never existed. And if you also place that savings in a place where it will grow, then you have a doubly powerful seed.

There's a kind of security that no job, no salary, no degree gives you. Only savings. Knowing you can cover three months, six months, or a year without income changes your life. It gives you the courage to make difficult decisions. To leave a job that no longer makes you happy. To start a project. To say no to what you don't want. Savings are the emotional reserve that allows you to live with dignity, without the constant fear that everything will fall apart.

It's also important to have a goal. Saving just for the sake of saving can be difficult. But if you're clear about why you're doing it, it becomes easier. It could be an emergency fund, a down payment on a house, a trip, an early retirement. Whatever it is, as long as it makes sense for you. That way, every time you save money, you'll feel like you're building something. That it's not a sacrifice, but an investment in your peace of mind.

And don't forget that saving is also about resisting. It's about saying no to consumerism. It's about breaking with the idea that you always need more. That everything is solved by buying. That spending is about enjoying. It's not true. True enjoyment often lies in knowing you can live well without spending so much. That you have control. That you don't need to fill emptiness with objects. That your happiness doesn't depend on what's in your shopping cart.

The people who achieve great things aren't always the ones who earn the most, but the ones who save the most. Those who knew how to postpone the reward. Those who understood that every penny saved is a building block in their future freedom. Because money saved is more than just a sum in the bank. It's the ability to breathe when others are drowning. It's the calm in the midst of chaos. It's that sigh of relief when the world is falling apart but you're ready.

So start today. Save something. Even if it's a little. Even if it seems insignificant. Even if you say, "This is useless." It helps. Of course it helps. Because you're training your mind. You're creating a habit. You're telling yourself that your future matters. And if you do this every day, without fail, one day you'll look back and be grateful you were so prudent. Because those who save as if they were going to end up with nothing, in the end, are the ones who have more. More money, more options, more freedom. And above all, more peace.

Never Depend on a Single Source of Income

Relying on a single source of income is like walking a tightrope without a net underneath. As long as everything is working, you can feel comfortable, but all it takes is one change, a crisis, or a decision beyond your control, and everything can suddenly come crashing down. It's a very fragile position, even if it seems comfortable. Having a single source of income means entrusting your entire financial well-being to one thing. And when that thing fails, there's nothing to sustain you. That's why one of the most important rules of money is to diversify your income. Don't put all your eggs in one basket. Because if the basket falls, you lose everything.

Many people believe that having a steady job is enough. That as long as they get paid each month, there's nothing to worry about. But jobs aren't permanent. Neither are businesses. Not even health. Everything that depends on a single source has an expiration date or risk of interruption. And if the day that source disappears, you don't have a backup plan, you're going to feel the blow very hard. That's why it's so important to create other avenues for income, even if they're small at first.

The big mistake is thinking that only the rich can have multiple sources of income. But it's the other way around. It's the people who seek to have more than one source of income who end up rich. And that doesn't mean you have to have ten businesses. Sometimes all it takes is an extra online sale, a service you offer on weekends, a property you rent, an investment that yields returns, or a talent that can be monetized. There are a thousand ways. The important thing is to start. Even if it's with something small. Even if it only yields a few pesos. Because what starts small, with perseverance, can become gigantic.

A second source of income not only gives you more money, it also gives you more peace of mind. It gives you space. It lets you breathe. Because you know that if one door closes, another one is open. And you're not at the mercy of just one thing. You don't need to beg a boss or stay in a place you hate just because it's your only source of income. You can choose. You can move. You can take risks. Diversification gives you personal power. And that power is worth gold.

There are people who work incredibly hard, even overtime, but all that effort is concentrated on a single source. What happens if they lose that job or that client? All the effort disappears. On the other hand, if that same effort were distributed to build other income sources, even small ones, the impact would be very different. Every extra income is a stronger root. It's stability. It's the future.

Additional income can come from very simple things. If you know something others want to learn, you can teach classes. If you have something others want to buy, you can sell it. If you like writing, recording videos, designing, cooking, fixing things, cleaning, translating, helping, or accompanying others, you can turn that into money. Today, more than ever, there are tools to monetize almost any skill. The hard part isn't doing it; the hard part is making the decision to start.

At first, that new income probably won't be much. It may not even seem worth it. But don't underestimate the power of growth. When a second source starts to grow, it becomes a foundation for more. Extra income gives you capital, and that capital can be invested elsewhere. And that's how a network of income is created. One supports the other. When one goes down, another makes up for it. And that's true financial stability: when you're not dependent on anyone or anything in particular, but on a whole that sustains you.

Furthermore, diversifying your income also trains your mind. It forces you to think differently. To step out of your comfort zone. To explore new things. It makes you a more creative, more flexible, and more prepared person. And that preparation not only gives you more money, it also makes you grow as a person. Because every new source of income is an opportunity to learn something you didn't know before. And that, in the long run, is worth more than any monthly check.

It's also important to clarify that not all sources of income have to require your time.

Some can be automated. A course you record once and sell many times. An online store that works with the help of suppliers. A well-placed investment. This is called passive income, and it's one of the most powerful types. Because while you sleep, work, or travel, the money keeps coming in. And that's real freedom.

Having multiple sources of income isn't just a financial strategy; it's a way of life. It's understanding that your future shouldn't depend on a single decision, a single company, a single client, or a single channel. It's spreading the risk. It's winning in multiple directions. It's stopping living in fear of something ending. Because if something ends, you move on. Because you have other paths open to you. Because you've thought about the future starting today.

So if you only have one source of income today, make a promise to yourself: start building another. Not tomorrow. Today. No matter how small. Do it with what you know, with what you have, with what you can. Take the first step. That little extra income can be the difference between living on the edge or living peacefully. Between always being dependent or having options. Between feeling trapped or feeling free. And that's priceless.

Invest Early, Even if It's Little

Investing is a word that sounds big, distant, and complicated. Most people think it's only for millionaires, financial experts, or people on TV talking about stocks and shares. But the truth is, investing doesn't have to be difficult or unattainable. Investing is simply putting your money to work for you, instead of you working all the time for it. And most importantly, the earlier you start, even with a little, the greater the results can be over time.

Many people put off investing. They say they don't have enough money, that it's not the right time, that they'll do it when they earn more. But that's like saying you're not going to plant a tree until you have a forest. The tree starts small and grows over the years. That's also how investment works. If you plant a little today, with perseverance and patience, that little can become a lot. Not by magic, but by something very powerful called compound interest. It's like a snowball that rolls and grows faster and faster; it just needs time and a little initial push.

The difference between investing early and late isn't just a matter of years; it's thousands, sometimes millions, of pesos. A person who invests 100 pesos a month from age 20, and does so until age 50, could have much more money than someone who invests 1,000 pesos a month but starts at age 40. Time is the key factor. When you invest young, you give your money more years to grow. And the older it is, the stronger it becomes. So it doesn't matter if you can only invest a little at first. What matters is that you start as early as possible.

Investing doesn't have to be risky or complicated. Today, there are many options for beginners. You can start with automated investment accounts, index funds, platforms that allow you to buy fractional shares, bond investments, mutual funds, or even more personal projects like starting your own small business. What you need to understand is that investing isn't the same as spending. When you spend, money disappears. When you invest well, money transforms, grows, and multiplies.

Another common mistake is thinking you need to understand everything before you start. That's like not wanting to go into the ocean until you know how to swim like a pro. The logical thing is to learn in the process. Read, ask questions, and inform yourself little by little. You don't need to be an expert to get started. You need willpower, commitment, and vision. And of course, it's always important to understand the risk, because every investment involves it. But there are also risks in not investing. Like working your whole life and never accruing anything. Like always depending on a salary. Like reaching old age without any support.

When you don't invest, you're letting your money lose value every year. Because inflation, even if you can't see it, slowly erodes your money's purchasing power. What you buy for 100 pesos today will cost 110 pesos tomorrow. And if your money doesn't grow at the same rate as that increase, you're becoming poorer without even realizing it. Investing is a way to protect yourself. To maintain the value of your efforts. To protect what you worked so hard to earn.

You must also understand that investing doesn't always mean just money. You can invest in learning something new, in a course, in a skill that you can later monetize. That's also an investment. Investing in yourself is often the best decision. Because you are your main wealth generator. And the more you are worth, the more you can generate, the more you can contribute, the more you can earn.

A great advantage of starting small is that you learn without putting into play amounts that hurt you. You can experiment, make mistakes, and improve. It's like a personal laboratory where you test and grow. And as you do, you develop the mindset of an investor. Someone who thinks about the future. Someone who doesn't seek immediate gratification, but rather long-term results. That mindset is what will separate you from those who always live day to day, who only think about spending today and regretting it tomorrow.

The investment journey is like a long walk. It's not about running, it's about never stopping. Every month you invest a little more, you're making progress. And the best part is that there comes a point where the money you invested starts generating more money on its own. It no longer depends on you working longer hours. That's freedom. That's financial intelligence. That's living with peace of mind, knowing you're building something solid.

So don't stop because you think it's not enough. Invest early, even if it's a small amount. The important thing is to develop the habit. To get used to thinking about sowing in order to reap. To ensure that every time you get paid, a portion goes toward your future. Not into oblivion, not into idleness, but into growth. Make it automatic if you can. Let investing become as natural as breathing. And you'll see how, over time, that small decision can completely change your life.

Because in the end, those who have a good relationship with money aren't those who earn the most, but those who know how to use it well. Those who understand that every peso you don't spend, every peso you invest, is a promise to your future self. A promise that says: I won't leave you alone, I'll take care of you starting today. And that, more than any luxury, is the true meaning of wealth.

Compound Interest is Your Best Friend

Compound interest is one of those things that seems boring at first, like a math formula no one wants to understand. But if you understand it well, it can become one of your greatest allies in life. It's like that silent friend who works for you every day, even while you sleep, without you having to do anything extra. And over time, it can give you something very few achieve: financial freedom. Most people don't value it because they don't understand it. But in the world of money, understanding compound interest is like having a flashlight in the dark.

Let's explain it simply. Compound interest is when your savings generate earnings, and those earnings, instead of being spent, are reinvested to continue generating more earnings. That is, you earn not only on your initial money, but also on what that money has already earned. It's like a snowball that grows faster the longer it rolls. At first, it grows slowly, almost unnoticeable. But if you're patient and let it roll for many years, it reaches a point where it begins to grow at an impressive speed.

For example, if you invest 1,000 pesos and it earns you 10 percent each year, at the end of the first year you'll have 1,100. If you leave that money untouched, the following year you won't earn just 100 pesos, but 110, because now you're earning on 1,100, not 1,000. And so on. Every year, the money you earn also starts earning more money. You're not doing anything new, you're not working anymore, but your money is. It works for you, multiplying itself. That's the magic of compound interest.

Now, the most powerful thing about compound interest isn't the amount you invest, but the time you give it. Someone who invests a little, but starts young, can end up with more money than someone who invests a lot, but starts late. Why? Because the first few years are the most important. They're what give that snowball momentum so it doesn't stop later on. That's why the sooner you start, even if it's just a little, the better. Compound interest takes time, like a seed that grows slowly but steadily. Don't rush it. Let it work.

One of the most important things you can do is always reinvest your earnings. Don't touch your money. Let it grow. The mistake many make is that as soon as they see a bit of profit, they withdraw it and spend it. That's killing the magic. That's pulling out the plant as it's barely begun to sprout. If you really want to see the power of compound interest, you have to commit to the long term. Let that money grow for years. Not one, not two. We're talking ten, twenty, thirty years. And if you're consistent, the results will surprise you.

This concept doesn't just apply to the money you invest in an account or fund. It can also be applied to your education, your habits, and your relationships. If you improve one percent each day at something, that one percent, over time, accumulates exponentially. Because each improvement builds on the previous one. And that, like financial compound interest, can take you much further than you imagine. But it's especially powerful with money, because while you go about your normal life, your money continues to grow in the background.

Compound interest also teaches you a great life lesson: that great things don't happen all at once, but are built on small decisions repeated many times. That perseverance trumps intensity. That those who start early and keep at it go further than those who start late with more energy. That patience is worth gold. Literally.

Of course, all of this only works if you have discipline. If you're not withdrawing money every time a craving strikes. If you don't let yourself get carried away by impatience. Because the greatest enemy of compound interest is impatience. We live in an age where we want everything now, fast, immediate. But smart money doesn't grow that way. It grows like a tree: steady, slow, but sure. You decide whether you want to eat seeds today or reap enormous rewards tomorrow.

For compound interest to work in your favor, you need to create the habit of investing consistently. It doesn't matter if it's just a little. The important thing is that you don't stop. That you put something in every month. That you make it a routine like brushing your teeth or paying the rent. Because that habit, even if it seems small, is what builds great fortunes over the years. The difference isn't in how much you earn, but in what you do with it.

Another key factor is choosing your investment wisely. It's not about putting your money anywhere. You have to research, compare, and understand the risks. Look for safe places with a good track record that allow you to reinvest your profits. And be aware that you may not see great results in the first few years. But don't get discouraged. The important thing isn't what you see now, but what you're building for later. It's like planting seeds. For a long time, you only see the soil. But one day, suddenly, you have a tree full of fruit.

So, if you're thinking about your future today, if you want freedom, if you want to sleep soundly knowing your money is growing on its own, start building that relationship with compound interest. Treat it like a friend. Give it time, respect it, nurture it, and it will return the favor in spades. And remember this powerful idea: compound interest can do more for you than any pay raise, any luck in life. Because it doesn't depend on anyone else, only on you and your perseverance.

Some people say that compound interest is the eighth wonder of the world. It may sound exaggerated, but when you experience it firsthand, when you see how your money transforms, you understand why they say it. Because in a world where almost everything depends on working harder, compound interest teaches you that there's another way: working smarter. And that, in the end, is the way that wins.

Watch Your Ant Expenses (They're Eating You Alive)

There are things in life that don't seem like a problem until they accumulate. Like a leak that slowly drips from the ceiling, which doesn't bother you at first, but if you don't fix it, it ends up filling an entire bucket or ruining the paint on the wall. These are the small expenses. Small, almost invisible, seemingly harmless. But if you don't control them, they can eat up a good portion of your money without you even realizing it. And the worst part is that most people don't notice them until it's too late.

An ant expense is that small, daily or frequent expense you make without much thought. It's not as big as rent, nor does it sound as important as insurance. It's the coffee you buy every morning on the go. It's the snack you put in your cart in line at the supermarket. It's the subscription to that platform you don't even use anymore, but that keeps getting discounted month after month. It's the app order you got because you were too lazy to cook. It's that craving you didn't need but bought anyway. They're small things, yes, but when they add up, they add up to a sum that can hurt.

Let's do a simple calculation. Let's say you spend thirty pesos a day on trivial things: a coffee, a cookie, a soda. Thirty pesos seems like nothing. But if you do that every day, by month that's nine hundred. And by year, ten thousand eight hundred pesos. What if you spend fifty a day? Or more? Do you realize how something so small can become a giant drain? That's what happens with small expenses. You don't notice them individually, but together they can drain your wallet.

The most dangerous thing about these expenses is that they're disguised as convenience. No one feels bad about buying a coffee. No one worries about paying for that music app, even if they don't listen to it anymore. The problem is that you get used to it. You do it without thinking. It becomes part of your routine. And the worst part is that you often do them on impulse, out of habit, out of boredom, or out of anxiety. Not because you really need to.

To take care of your money, you first have to be aware of where it's going. Write down all your small expenses for a week. All of them, without any filter. From a piece of gum to a taxi you took out of laziness. At the end of the week, review that list. You'll be surprised. You'll see how much money you're wasting on things that don't really contribute anything to your life. And once you see it with your own eyes, there's no excuse. You can no longer say you didn't know.

The solution isn't to stop enjoying life. It's not about living like a monk or eliminating all joy. It's about choosing. Deciding what you do want to spend money on and what isn't worth it. Maybe you really enjoy that Friday coffee, and it makes you happy. Great, save it. But maybe the other four days you could bring one from home. Or switch to a cheaper option. It's not about stopping living, but about stopping wasting money without realizing it.

It's also important to automate what's important. If you already have a budget where you define how much you can spend on certain things, it will be easier not to go overboard. You can even have a separate account for personal expenses, and when that money runs out, it's gone. That way, you don't touch what's meant for savings or toward your goals. And over time, you'll become more aware of your habits. More responsible. Smarter with your money.

A very useful trick is to turn those small expenses into investments. If you normally spend fifty pesos a day on unnecessary things, try saving that same amount in a separate account. Call this account your "anti-ant fund." At the end of the month, you'll have fifteen hundred pesos that you can use for something that actually brings you closer to your goals: paying off a debt, investing, buying something you really need, or simply treating yourself to a more enjoyable experience that's worthwhile.

The point is that money doesn't just go away. It escapes where you let it. And if you don't plug those small leaks, it doesn't matter how much you earn. You'll always feel like it's not enough. Because every peso that goes for no reason is a peso not used to grow. Every small expense you don't control is a missed opportunity to build a stronger future. Because in the end, the difference between someone who thrives and someone who stagnates isn't always in the big expenses, but in the small details that add up or subtract every day.

Don't be fooled by the small things. One ant isn't scary. But a thousand can eat up an entire house. That's what happens with your money. If you don't pay attention, they'll drain your wallet while you continue to think you're fine. So open your eyes, review your habits, make smart adjustments, and start putting the brakes on those small decisions that are keeping you from a more peaceful life. Because when you learn to control the small things, you're one step closer to controlling the big things. And that's what makes the difference between living with anxiety or with freedom.

Learn to Say NO

One of the most powerful, yet underappreciated, skills when it comes to money is knowing how to say no. No to unnecessary purchases. No to outings you can't afford. No to loans you know you won't get back. No to the temptations that appear every day disguised as sales, emergencies, or social pressure. Saying no isn't being stingy. It's not being a bad person. It's simply protecting your present and your financial future. It's being clear about what you want, and what you're not willing to sacrifice.

The problem is that we live in a culture where saying yes has become almost an obligation. Saying yes makes you look good, makes you feel part of something, makes you seem generous or fun. But often, that "yes" you say is a "no" to your peace of mind. Sometimes that "yes" costs you dearly. Sometimes that "yes" puts you in debt, stresses you out, or distances you from your goals. And the worst part is that it happens so quickly, so automatically, that you don't even realize it. And then you wonder why you can't afford it, why you feel like you're working and not making progress. And often, the answer lies in those unnecessary "yeses" you said because you didn't want to upset others.

Saying no is uncomfortable, of course it is. No one likes to be the one who breaks the plan, the one who says "I'll pass," the one who doesn't jump on the collective spending bandwagon. But if you learn to do it intelligently, you'll save yourself a lot of headaches. Because every time you say no to something you don't need, you're saying yes to your stability. To your savings. To your goals. To your peace. And that, even if it's not visible at the time, is worth much more than any dinner, any fad, any impulse purchase.

Think of it this way: every financial decision you make is an investment or a loss. And often, the simple act of not spending is one of the best investments you can make. Because it's not just about earning more money, but learning to take care of the money you already have. And for that, you need limits. And limits are built with noes. With conscious decisions. With the courage to resist what's easy, what's popular, what's immediate.

Sometimes the most important no isn't to others, but to yourself. Saying no to your cravings. To your impulsiveness. To your need to pretend. To your habit of saying "I deserve it" when you don't really need it. It's not about living with guilt, but with awareness. It's not about not being able to indulge yourself; it's about learning to choose which ones are truly worth it and which ones are just sabotaging you.

You also have to learn to say no when someone asks you for a loan and you know they won't pay you back. It's hard, because it's often someone close to you. But you have to understand that helping doesn't always mean giving. Sometimes the best way to help is to say no, especially if it puts your own stability at risk. You can't save others by sinking yourself. You can't please everyone and at the same time take care of your finances. You have to choose. And that takes courage.

Even at work, knowing how to say no can help you earn more. Sometimes you accept unfair conditions, low-paying jobs, or clients who demand too much because you're afraid to say no. But when you learn to value yourself, to set boundaries, and to reject what isn't good for you, you also begin to make room for what is good. Sometimes, a well-said no leads to a much bigger yes.

Now, it's not about saying no with arrogance or rudeness. You can say no with respect, with firmness, with honesty. A no said clearly is better than a yes filled with resentment or anguish. And the best part is that the more you practice, the easier it becomes. It's hard at first, because the body is trained to please. But over time, you learn to enjoy the power of decision. Of taking control.

Many people live in debt not because of big decisions, but because of small "yeses" they didn't know how to refuse in time. A weekend plan. A pressured purchase. A trip they couldn't afford. A subscription they never canceled. And so, one after another, these things dragged them down. But you can change that. You can train yourself to view every invitation, every opportunity to spend, as a question that deserves an honest answer. Is this bringing me closer to or further from my goal? If it's taking you further away, the answer should be no. Period.

Saying no is uncomfortable only at first. Then comes freedom. Then comes the peace of mind of knowing you're being consistent with yourself, with what you want, with what you need. And that consistency, even if it's not apparent at the moment, is what builds a healthy financial life.

So, the next time you feel that pressure to say yes, breathe. Think about what really matters. And if you have to say no, say it. Calmly. Firmly. Wisely. Because that no, however small it may seem, can be the first step toward a lighter, freer, and much smarter life.

Stop Pretending

There's a very common trap that many people fall into without realizing it: the need to pretend. Pretending to have more, to be better, to pretend to be successful, to have wealth, or to have a perfect life that doesn't really exist. And the saddest thing about this trap is that it's often paid for with money you don't have, with accumulated stress, and with dreams postponed because you're focused on impressing others. Pretending not only empties your pockets, it also empties your authenticity.

And why do we do it? Because we live in a society obsessed with image. Social media is full of people showing off what they buy, where they travel, what clothes they wear, what car they drive. And even if they don't say it openly, the message is clear: if you don't have that, you're not worth that much. And if you don't show it, you don't exist. This puts us in an invisible competition to show off, to appear, to upload a photo, to tell others what we buy, to live more for the eyes of others than for ourselves.

The problem is that trying to pretend has a cost. And that cost is often very high. It's spending money on things you don't need. It's going into debt to buy a new phone when the one you have still works. It's going to expensive restaurants when you could eat better and healthier at home. It's buying designer clothes just to feel like you belong. It's taking vacations you can't afford, just to say you were there. And while you're doing all of this to impress, inside you're emptying yourself.

One of the most liberating decisions you can make is to stop pretending. To stop living for the approval of others. To stop feeling like you have to prove something. Because true financial freedom isn't built on what people think you have, but on what you really have. On what you save. On what you invest. On what you build for the long term, even if it doesn't show in a photo.

Many true millionaires don't look like it. They don't lavish themselves with luxuries, own fancy cars, or wear clothes that scream brand names. Because they've already understood that wealth doesn't require proof. It's those who want to appear rich who spend the most. It's those who don't have anything, but want others to believe they do, who get into financial trouble. And it's very easy to fall into that trap if you're not careful.

Living for show keeps you away from your real goals. It keeps you away from saving, investing, having an emergency fund, paying off your debts, and growing your wealth. Because all your money goes into maintaining an image that doesn't even make you happy. And when a crisis, an emergency, or a real opportunity comes, you have nothing to respond with, because you've already written everything down on yourself, or on a maxed-out credit card.

The ironic thing is that most of the people you want to impress don't even care that much about you. They're busy with their own lives, their own problems, their own appearances. So you spend money to impress people who probably don't care, while you bear the consequences. Is it worth it? No. It never has been.

Stop pretending doesn't mean living in scarcity. It means living consciously. Knowing that you don't need to prove your worth through objects. That your peace of mind is worth more than the validation of others. That your peace of mind is priceless. That it's better to have money in the bank than designer clothes in your closet. That a reliable, paid-for car is better than a luxurious one with monthly payments that suffocate you. That it's better to be discreet and free than noisy and in debt.

Learning to live below your means isn't a weakness, it's a strategy. It's understanding that if you can spend a thousand today, but choose to spend five hundred, you're building a stronger future. You're giving yourself room to grow, to invest, to have options. You're gaining control. And that's far more valuable than any appearance.

So the next time you're tempted to buy something just so others can see you're capable, ask yourself: Do I want it, or do I just want to be seen with it? Do I need it, or am I trying to fill an emotional void? Is this bringing me closer to or further from the life I truly want? If the answer isn't right for you, then save that money. Use it for something meaningful. Something that gives you peace, stability, and real power.

Because when you stop pretending, you start living seriously. And then you discover that you don't need so much to be well. That there's no pressure when you're not competing with anyone. That true wealth is seen in your peace of mind, not in your things. That having less, if managed well, can be much more than pretending to have it all. And that's where true abundance begins.

Money is Not bad, it is a Tool

For centuries, money has had a bad reputation. Many people grew up hearing phrases like money is the root of all evil or people with money are selfish and corrupt. These ideas, as harsh as they may sound, have become ingrained in the collective subconscious and have led many people to view money as something dirty, something dangerous, or something to be kept away from in order to be a good person. But the truth is, money isn't bad. Money, in reality, is just a tool. Like a knife, a hammer, a telephone. It's neither good nor bad in and of itself. What changes everything is how you use it.

A knife can be used to cut bread and feed your family, or it can be used to cause harm. The knife isn't to blame. The person who uses it is. The same thing happens with money. There are people who, with money, build hospitals, help communities, create businesses that provide jobs, support their families, and live in peace. And there are others who, with money, destroy, manipulate, or become slaves to their own excesses. But money isn't the villain. It's just an amplifier. It brings out what's already inside each of us.

Thinking that money is bad is one of the most limiting beliefs you can have if you want to move forward in life. Because if you see money as an enemy, you'll push it away. You'll sabotage yourself every time you start earning more. You'll feel guilty for wanting to improve your situation. You'll reject opportunities. You'll live with a sense of internal conflict that doesn't allow you to grow. And all because of a misconception. Because of a belief that doesn't help you.

Now, when you start seeing money as a tool, everything changes. You realize that having money doesn't make you a bad person. It makes you a person with more options. More freedom. More ability to decide. Because money doesn't buy happiness, but it does buy time. It does reduce stress. It does allow you to help. It does allow you to choose how to live. When you don't have money, everything is urgent. Everything is worry. Everything is about survival. But when you have control over your money, you can begin to live with intention, not just need.

Imagine you're building a house. What would you do it with faster and with less effort? With your bare hands or with tools? The same thing happens in life. Money isn't the goal, but it can be the bridge. The one that takes you from where you are to where you want to be. It's not the most important thing, but it does make a big difference. Because money well spent can give you health, it can give you education, it can give you security, it can give you unforgettable experiences, and, above all, it can give you peace of mind.

The problem isn't having money. The problem is not knowing how to use it. It's putting money above your values. It's becoming a slave to money instead of making it work for you. It's losing control, it's getting into debt, it's living for show. But none of this is caused by money. It's caused by a bad relationship with it. And you can change that relationship. You can decide to see money as an ally. As a resource you learn to manage. As a tool that helps you live better.

Furthermore, when you have a good relationship with money, you don't just improve your life, you can also improve the lives of others. Because a person with money and a good heart can do a lot of good. They can donate, they can invest in worthy causes, they can support their family, they can create jobs, they can offer stability to those around them. Well-managed money not only transforms your bank account, it can also transform the environment. It can change realities.

Many people say they'd rather be happy without money than unhappy with it. And that's fine. No one is saying money is everything. But why not both? Why not be happy and have money? Why not live with purpose and at the same time have financial stability? They're not opposites. In fact, they often go hand in hand. Because when you're not burdened by bills, you can think more clearly. You can pursue what you love. You can enjoy your loved ones more. You can have quality time. And all of that is also part of happiness.

So if you've ever felt that money was evil, if you've ever thought that being poor made you more noble, if you've ever rejected the possibility of prosperity for fear of change, it's time to rethink that idea. Because as long as you continue to see money as something dirty, it will be very difficult for it to come to you. And if it does, it will be difficult for it to stay. But if you see it for what it is—a powerful tool that you can learn to use—then you'll be ready to build a fuller, freer, and more abundant life.

And that's the simplest truth we sometimes forget: money isn't the problem. The problem is how we understand it. How we use it. How we relate to it. But once you understand it, once you stop being afraid of it, you can start using it to your advantage. And that's where your true financial freedom begins.

Good Debt Makes You Rich, Bad Debt Sinks You

The word debt has a bad reputation. When we hear it, many people think of worry, anxiety, unpaid bills, calls from banks, snowballing interest rates, and sleepless nights. And no wonder. Many people have sunk into debt due to poor decisions or a lack of understanding of how money works. But the funny thing is, not all debt is bad. In fact, there are debts that can make you rich. Yes, even if it sounds strange. The difference is knowing which one is which. Because there is good debt that works for you, and there is bad debt that works against you. One helps you build, the other leads you to disaster.

Bad debt is the most common type. It's the debt you take on to buy things you don't need, with money you don't have, to impress people you don't even care about. It's when you buy a new cell phone with a credit card just because the latest model came out, even though yours still works. It's when you take out a loan to go on vacation, but then spend a whole year paying interest for a week of pleasure. It's when you pay the minimum on your card and let the interest accumulate as if nothing happened. This debt is dangerous because it feeds on impulse, a lack of planning, and a constant desire to live beyond your means. This debt enslaves you.

Bad debt doesn't just affect your wallet; it also affects your mind. It robs you of your peace. It steals your sleep. It makes you work only to pay, not to grow. It forces you to make decisions out of fear. It puts you on a never-ending cycle, always owing, owing, owing. And the worst part is that you often don't even know exactly how much you owe. You just know that you can't afford it, that you're living on the edge, that you collect and you already owe everything. That's no life. That's surviving tied to an invisible chain.

But now let's talk about the other side of the coin: good debt. That debt exists, and it has a very different purpose. Good debt is debt you take on intelligently, that has a strategy behind it, that you use to generate more money than you're borrowing. It's when you take out a loan to start a business that already has clients and guaranteed sales. It's when you buy a property to rent out, and the rent covers the loan payment, even leaving some profit. It's when you study a degree that you know will double your salary in a few years. That debt doesn't sink you, it propels you. It's like a lever that allows you to achieve things you couldn't with your savings alone.

The key to a good debt lies in three things: that it has a clear return, that the return is greater than what you're going to pay, and that you can cover it without suffocating yourself. If a debt meets these conditions, it can be your best ally. Because it's not about being afraid of owing, but rather knowing what you're owing for. If you approach it with a cool head, with numbers in hand, a payment plan, and a realistic income projection, that debt becomes an investment. And that's when it starts working in your favor.

Most wealthy people have used good debt at some point. They didn't become millionaires just by saving. They used other people's money, but wisely. They knew that if they took out a loan to grow, and that growth left them with more money than they had borrowed, they were winning. It's like using the bank's money to build a ladder, and with that ladder, you reach higher than you could on your own legs. Of course, you have to be careful. You have to know how to measure. But if you do it right, it works.

So, the next time you think about going into debt, ask yourself these questions: Is this going to give me more money than I'm borrowing? Can I pay off this debt without going hungry or living in a state of distress? Am I investing or just satisfying a whim? If the answers aren't clear, it's best to wait. But if you see a real, analyzed, and profitable opportunity, then that debt can be a tool to move forward.

It's not about living in fear of debt. It's about understanding it. Mastering it. Using it like fire. Fire can cook your food or burn down your house. It all depends on how you handle it. The same thing happens with debt. If you learn to identify good debt and avoid bad debt, you'll be taking one of the most important steps toward improving your financial life. Don't become a slave to impulsive spending. Instead, become a strategic decision-maker.

Money has its rules, and one of the clearest is this: not all debt is bad, but bad debt is the most common. That's why you have to be alert. You have to observe carefully before signing. Because a signature can sink you or it can lift you up. And the difference lies in knowing whether that debt is a burden or an investment. You choose which side to be on.

Protect your Money

Earning money is only half the battle. The other half, the one many forget, is protecting it. Because it's pointless to work, save, or invest if that money later slips away due to carelessness, mistakes, or bad decisions. Protecting your money is like caring for a plant you've planted with effort. If you don't water it, if you don't monitor it, if you don't protect it from the sun, the wind, or pests, it won't matter how well it grew at first. It will eventually wither. The same thing happens with money. If you don't protect it, someone or something will take it. And you won't even realize it until it's too late.

Protecting your money isn't just about hiding it under the mattress or putting it all in a bank account. It's about having the mindset that money, even if it's with you, is never completely safe. There are scams, there are bad investments, there are impulsive decisions, there are friends who borrow and don't pay back, there are credit cards that go haywire, there are robberies, there are unexpected events, there are illnesses, there are emergencies. Life is full of unexpected moments that can leave you penniless if you're not prepared. And that's what this rule is for: to remind you that your money needs protection.

The first way to protect your money is with information. The less you know, the easier it is for someone to steal it from you. That's why you have to read, learn, and ask questions. You have to understand how banks, taxes, investments, and insurance work. No one has to be a financial expert, but we should all have a basic understanding of how money moves. Because when you know, you're not so easily fooled. You don't sign up for anything. You don't invest in strange schemes just because someone promises to double your money in a week. You don't hand over your savings to anyone in a suit and a smile. Knowledge is a barrier against thieves disguised as opportunities.

The second way is to be cautious. Having an emergency fund, for example, is a way to protect yourself and your money. If you're suddenly laid off, get sick, your car breaks down, or any unexpected expense arises, having that cushion prevents you from going into debt or emptying your investments. That fund should be sacred. It should be in a safe, yet accessible place. And it should cover at least three to six months of your fixed expenses. It's not a luxury to have. It's a necessity if you want to sleep soundly.

The third way to protect your money is with insurance. Many people view insurance as an unnecessary expense until they need it. And when they do, they're grateful they had it. Good health insurance can save you from unpayable debt for an operation. Car insurance can prevent you from paying thousands for an accident. Life insurance can protect your family if something happens to you. Insurance isn't for the faint of heart. It's for responsible people. No one wants something bad to happen, but if it does, it's better to be prepared.

Another way to protect your money is to not lend it so easily. It sounds harsh, but it's true. Many people lose their money not to thieves, but to friends and family who borrow and never repay. The problem isn't just the money that's lost, but the relationship that's broken. So, if you're going to lend, make it an amount you can afford to lose without resentment. And if you can't afford that, simply learn to say no. Your financial stability shouldn't be shaken by someone else's liability.

You must also protect your money from yourself. From your impulses, from your urge to buy without thinking, from your emotions that sometimes lead you to spend out of anxiety, sadness, or boredom. The mind can be your worst enemy when it comes to money. That's why it's important to have clarity. To have goals. To know what you're saving, investing, and earning for. That clarity stops you from spending just because you had a bad day. And it also helps you distinguish between what's urgent and what's important.

And let's not forget protection against time. Inflation, for example, is that silent enemy that makes your money worth less each year if it's stagnant. If you keep everything under the mattress or in an account that doesn't earn anything, you can buy less each year with the same amount. That's why protecting your money also means moving it wisely. Investing it. Putting it to work.

Because money sitting still loses value. But money well-placed grows.

In short, protecting your money is an act of self-love. It's respecting your efforts. It's caring for what you've worked hard to build. It's not about living in fear, but about living intelligently. About making decisions with the future in mind, not just the present. About understanding that the money you don't take care of, someone else will take advantage of. And that the difference between moving forward or backward often isn't how much you earn, but how much you manage to keep. So protect yourself. Protect yourself from ignorance, carelessness, excess, opportunists, and yourself. Because in this world, unprotected money disappears. And when it disappears, starting over is harder. But if you take good care of it today, that money can open many doors for you tomorrow. And that, believe me, is worth the effort.

Learn to Sell Something (Even if It's Just an Idea)

Knowing how to sell is one of the most powerful skills you can have in life. It doesn't matter if you don't have a business, if you're not a salesperson, if you've never worked in sales. Sooner or later, you'll have to sell something. It could be a product, a service, your experience, your talent, or even an idea. In fact, we all sell something, even if we don't call it that. When you do a job interview, you're selling your profile. When you make a proposal to a partner, you're selling a vision of the future. When you motivate a friend, you're selling an idea. And when you post something on social media, you're selling an image of yourself. So, if we all sell, why not learn to do it well?

The problem is that many people associate the word "selling" with manipulation, deception, or pressure. But real selling has nothing to do with that. Selling is communicating value. It's getting someone to understand why something you offer can improve their life. It's connecting a need with a solution. It's listening, understanding, and proposing something that makes sense to the other person. And this, when done well, isn't just helpful. It's a way to build relationships, open doors, and change your financial situation forever.

If you learn to sell, you'll never run out of options. Because even if you lose everything you have, you can start over from scratch. If you know how to sell, you can offer anything and generate income. You can start a business, you can grow in your work, you can make alliances. Knowing how to sell makes you valuable anywhere, in any context. It's a skill that pays well because it moves the world. And even if you don't sell physical objects, the world needs people who know how to present ideas, projects, and solutions. That's selling. And that's something anyone can learn.

Selling well starts with knowing the person in front of you. You can't offer the same thing to everyone. Each person has a different story, a need, a different problem. The mistake many salespeople make is talking too much and listening too little. And that's the key: a good salesperson listens better. They understand what the other person really wants. And then they show them how what you have can help them. It's that simple. It's not about pressuring, but about connecting. It's not about convincing by force, but about making the other person see the value for themselves.

Now, if you say you have nothing to sell, stop and think again. Do you know how to cook? You can sell courses, recipes, experiences. Do you like to write? You can sell texts, stories, ideas. Are you good at organizing? You can sell your time, your planning skills. Everyone has something to offer. You just have to know how to present it attractively. And to do that, you need to learn how to communicate, how to express yourself clearly, how to show benefits, how to build trust. Because in the end, people don't just buy what you sell, they buy how you make them feel. They buy security, they buy results, they buy experience.

Even if what you want to sell is just an idea, you need the same tools. An idea isn't imposed, it's sown. And to sow it, you have to wrap it in words that resonate, in emotions that connect, in arguments that convince. Great leaders, great entrepreneurs, great innovators—all are, above all, great sellers of ideas. No one changes the world without first selling the world a new vision. So if you have an idea, no matter how small, start practicing how to tell it. How to explain it simply, how to make the other person care.

You don't have to become a sales genius overnight. But you should practice. Every day. Start with something simple. Offer a product or service you'd use yourself. Talk to friends, offer help, make exchanges. Observe what works and what doesn't. Learn from every conversation. Improve your presentation. Fine-tune your words. Be authentic, be honest, but don't be afraid to charge. Because selling is also about valuing yourself. It's also about understanding that your time, effort, and knowledge have a price. And that if they contribute something useful, they deserve to be compensated.

The reality is that money moves where there are sales. The world's largest companies sell. Influencers sell. Artists sell. Politicians sell. Everyone who has an impact has learned to communicate effectively. And if you want more freedom, more income, more opportunities, you need to learn too. It's not something exclusive to extroverts. It's not a gift reserved for a select few. It's a skill that can be trained, like any other. And the sooner you develop it, the sooner you'll see results.

It's not about rushing out and opening a store. It's about not getting caught up in the idea that selling is something foreign to you. Because selling is simply about clearly conveying value. And if you learn to do it, even with an idea, you're already one step closer to earning more, living better, and not depending on anyone. So start today. With what you have. With what you're good at. With what you enjoy. There will be mistakes, yes. But there will also be learnings. And with each attempt, you'll be sharpening one of the most powerful tools in existence: your ability to sell.

Be an Owner, Not an Employee

Throughout life, most people grow up with the idea that the right thing to do is to study hard, get a good job, earn a steady salary, and retire someday. And yes, there's nothing wrong with having a job. But if what you're looking for is financial freedom, true independence, and real control over your time, then you have to understand one thing that completely changes the way you view money: someone who works for a salary is always constrained by someone else. Someone who owns money, on the other hand, can build something that works for them.

Being an employee means exchanging your time for money. That is, you work eight, ten, or even more hours a day, and in return you receive a fixed salary, which often doesn't even reflect everything you do. It doesn't matter if you work hard or just do the bare minimum. The check arrives anyway. And that may sound comfortable, but it can also be a trap. Because that salary, no matter how high it seems, has a ceiling. It's limited by the decisions of others. And if one day that company closes, or there's a crisis, or they simply don't need you anymore, you're left with nothing.

When you're an owner, the rules change. You're no longer dependent on someone else hiring you. You don't need to ask permission to earn more. You decide how much you're worth, you decide what to build, you decide when to work and when to rest. It's not easy, of course. At first, it involves more effort, more risk, more uncertainty. But it's also more rewarding. Because everything you build as an owner—be it a business, an investment, or a personal brand—can grow without having to work longer hours. You can delegate, automate, scale. And that gives you something no salary can give you: freedom.

Many people think that being an owner means having a big company or a lot of employees. But that's not the case. Being an owner is a mindset. It's understanding that you can have control over your income. That you can start a business from home, from your phone, from something small. You can sell a product, a service, an idea. You can have an online store, a social media account that you monetize, a property that you rent, an app, a course. The options are endless, but it all begins when you stop thinking only as an employee and start thinking as an owner.

There are employees who make a lot of money, of course. But even they have a problem: if they stop working, they stop earning. On the other hand, when you own a system, that system can continue to function without you. A restaurant keeps selling even if you're not in the kitchen. A property keeps generating rent even if you're on vacation. A YouTube channel can continue to get views even if you don't upload new content for a while. That's what gives you long-term security. Because the real goal of money isn't just earning, it's earning without being present all the time.

This doesn't mean you should quit your job immediately. But it does mean you should start building something of your own right now. Use your job as a tool to finance your dreams, not as your final destination. Learn from what you see in your company: how they sell, how they handle customers, how they solve problems. And then apply it to your own. Because all the knowledge you acquire as an employee can help you become a better owner. The difference lies in the intention. An employee works out of obligation. An owner works out of vision.

The path of the owner is not linear. Sometimes you fail, sometimes you doubt, sometimes you feel like you're not moving forward. But each step brings you closer to a freer, richer, more personal life. It's not about becoming a millionaire overnight. It's about creating a source of income that doesn't depend solely on your time. That allows you to take care of your family, live at your own pace, and not depend on a boss, a company, or an external situation. It's about having options. Because the true power of money isn't in how much you have, but in how much freedom it gives you.

And remember something important: absolute security doesn't exist. Not even in the most stable job. The only real security is the one you build yourself. Ownership isn't for a select few. It's for anyone who's tired of dependency, who wants control, who's willing to learn, to try, to create something meaningful. So start wherever you are. Learn something new. Invest in yourself. Create something small. But don't wait for someone else to give you permission to move forward. Own your time, your income, and most of all, your life. Because when you understand this, you never think the way you did before. You start acting like someone who's already building their freedom. And that changes everything.

Money Goes Where There Is Order

Money doesn't like chaos. It doesn't like confusion, disorder, or uncertainty. Money is like an important visitor who only arrives when he knows he'll find a clean house, things clear, and an environment where he can relax. And this isn't a romantic metaphor; it's a very concrete reality: if you don't have order in your finances, money simply leaves. It slips through every crack. No matter how much you earn, if you don't know how to manage it, you'll always feel like it's not enough. Because the problem isn't how much comes in, it's how you manage it.

Order means knowing exactly how much you earn, how much you spend, what you spend it on, how much you owe, how much you save, and what you do with the extra. If you can't answer these questions clearly right now, you're probably losing money without realizing it. And it's not about having a perfect Excel spreadsheet or being an accountant. It's about knowing where your money is right now. Because if you don't know where your money is going, you'll never be able to control it.

Imagine your money is like water flowing through a pipe. If that pipe is broken, leaking everywhere, it doesn't matter how much water you put in: it's always going to be lost. On the other hand, if the pipe is well sealed, if everything is connected properly, even a small amount of water can go a long way. The same thing happens with your finances. If you're organized, you can do wonders even on a low income. But if you're disorganized, you'll drown with any amount of money. There are people who earn thousands and live life to the fullest. And there are others who earn little, yet have financial peace. The difference is in order.

Order also means having clear priorities. You can't spend on everything. You can't have everything at once. You have to decide. And when you know what you want, it's easier to decide what to spend on and what not to. Disorganized people tend to spend on impulse, buy without thinking, and go into debt for unnecessary things. Organized people think ahead, plan, and anticipate. Order isn't rigidity; it's applied intelligence. It's having control.

Another key point of order is emotional control. Because many financial disorders don't come from ignorance, but from emotions. Those who buy out of anxiety, sadness, social pressure, or habit often do so without thinking. And then they wonder why they can't afford it. Order is also emotional. It's learning to say no. It's understanding that you don't need to prove anything to anyone. It's recognizing when you're spending on a whim and when out of necessity.

And something that's sometimes forgotten: order brings peace. Knowing you have your finances in order, that you're not running after money, that every penny has a place and a purpose, gives you a peace of mind that's priceless. You live more lightly. You don't stress out every time the end of the month comes. You don't have to borrow or expect miracles. And that, even if you don't see it, gives you a huge advantage over the rest of the world.

If you're going through a tough time today, if you feel like you don't have enough, if you're in debt, the first thing you should do isn't earn more. It's sorting through what you already have. Because if you can't manage a hundred well, you won't manage a thousand either. And if you can't manage a thousand, you won't manage ten thousand either. Money amplifies what you already are. If you're disorganized, it will drag you down further. If you're organized, it will help you grow.

Start with the basics. Write down your income. Make a list of all your expenses, without lying to yourself. Identify which expenses are necessary and which are luxuries you could avoid for a while. Set a budget. Decide how much you're going to save, even if it's just a little. And most importantly: stick to that plan. Order isn't something you do once. It's a habit. It's a way of life.

You don't have to become a financial robot. You can indulge yourself, you can enjoy yourself, you can live well. But everything has to have a balance. Because money, when it sees structure, feels welcome. And when it feels welcome, it stays. Order isn't a punishment; it's the gateway to freedom.

And whoever learns to organize their money ends up organizing many other parts of their life as well. Because money, in the end, only follows the path where there is clarity, direction, and purpose. Where there is order, money multiplies. Where there is chaos, money disappears. It's that simple. It's that powerful.

www.ingramcontent.com/pod-product-compliance
Lightning Source LLC
La Vergne TN
LVHW090424210926
848480LV00002B/671
* 9 7 9 8 2 3 1 5 5 3 9 1 4 *